Reading Guide to *Moving into the Ecumenical Future*

Reading Guide to *Moving into the Ecumenical Future*

LOYES SPAYD

RESOURCE *Publications* · Eugene, Oregon

READING GUIDE TO MOVING INTO THE ECUMENICAL FUTURE

Copyright © 2025 Loyes Spayd. All rights reserved. Except for brief quotations in critical publications or reviews, no part of this book may be reproduced in any manner without prior written permission from the publisher. Write: Permissions, Wipf and Stock Publishers, 199 W. 8th Ave., Suite 3, Eugene, OR 97401.

Resource Publications
An Imprint of Wipf and Stock Publishers
199 W. 8th Ave., Suite 3
Eugene, OR 97401

www.wipfandstock.com

PAPERBACK ISBN: 979-8-3852-5524-5
HARDCOVER ISBN: 979-8-3852-5525-2
EBOOK ISBN: 979-8-3852-5526-9

07/03/25

Contents

The Crossin/Oblate Family Partnership | vii

Introduction | ix

Chapter 1 The Holy Spirit | 1

Chapter 2 Pastoral Ministry and Discernment | 3

Chapter 3 Biblical Ethics | 6

Chapter 4 Personal Relationships in a Relational Universe | 10

Chapter 5 Ecumenical Foundations / Dialogues | 14

Chapter 6 Moral Systems | 19

Chapter 7 Virtue Ethics Today | 23

Chapter 8 Moral Acts and the Promise of Peacebuilding | 27

Chapter 9 Ecumenical Reflections on Moral Discernment | 34

Chapter 10 An Ecumenical Paradigm for Moral Teaching | 44

Biographical History | 53

Sources | 55

A Note from Loyes Spayd | 57

The Crossin/Oblate Family Partnership

The family of Fr. John Crossin, OSFS, together with his Oblate brothers and colleagues in the ecumenical world, have joined together to honor his life's work. Since Fr. John's passing in 2023, a partnership has been formed to promote his publications and continue the ecumenical dialogue to which he dedicated this life. We share Fr. John's work through these initiatives:

- Promotion and distribution of Fr. John Crossin's most recent book, *Moving into the Ecumenical Future*
- A webpage with Fr. John's articles, publications, and videos www.oblates.org/living-the-legacy
- Symposium at Washington Theological Consortium featuring Fr. John's work (was held in April 2024)
- An annual high school ecumenism and unity essay contest
- Publication of a memorial volume focused on key themes of Fr. Crossin's scholarship *(in process)*
- Facebook Group "Moving in the Ecumenical Future"

Introduction

The Crossin/Oblate Partnership Team was formed after the death of Fr. John Crossin, OSFS, to carry on his work and promote the "Future" envisioned in his book, *Moving into the Ecumenical Future: Foundations of a Paradigm for Christian Ethics*. (To learn more about the Partnership Team visit www.oblates.org/living-the-legacy.) The team suggested that one of the many projects proposed to continue Fr. John's legacy was a Reading Guide to his book.

The goal of this guide is to assist Catholic parishioners, priests, students, seminarians, members of Ecumenical groups and any interested Christians with some of the history of ecumenicism and the progress accomplished over the last two centuries. Most importantly, though, is not only to read Fr. Crossin's book, but also to gather with other Christians, to learn, pray, grow spiritually, and listen to the Holy Spirit. Fr. John strongly recommends the latter, and to discern how best to move forward to make Fr. John's future a reality. No doubt this is a huge, daunting task, but great and often difficult events happen when a community listens to and cooperates with the wisdom and grace of the Holy Spirit! This guide and the book could be used in parish book clubs, discussion clubs, adult faith formation, prayer groups. It could be used as a course in the curriculum of Catholic High Schools, Catholic colleges and Universities, seminaries and divinity schools, ecumenical groups, diocesan groups, professional ecumenists and for any community interested in the pursuit of Christian unity.

Mitzi Budde, Professor Emerita, Virginia Theological Seminary, Alexandria, a colleague and dear friend of Fr. John's, wrote the foreword to his book and she summarizes its purpose:

Introduction

Father Crossin gently challenges all Christians to listen for the Spirit's guidance and "get out of ourselves and our worlds and encounter other Christians, learn from them, and become holy." (Ch.10) His invitation is to the church catholic; he addresses Roman Catholics, Lutherans, Methodists, Anglicans, Reformed, Orthodox, Baptists, and others.

If you are a Christian seeking to live your faith ethically in the twenty-first century in continuity with Scripture and the faith of the Church, this book is for you as well. In it you will encounter the voice of a wise teacher, an experienced pastor, a brilliant academician, an ecumenical enthusiast, and a discerning spiritual leader.

Mitzi Budde, Foreword to *Moving into the Ecumenical Future*, by Fr. John Crossin, OSFS, pp. viii, ix

CHAPTER 1

The Holy Spirit

OPENING PRAYER: Holy Spirit, open our minds and hearts to your promptings. Give us wisdom as we explore your role in the Trinity, in our lives, and in guiding the ecumenical movement.

BRIEF SUMMARY: Fr. Crossin explores the role of the Holy Spirit in the Trinity and the effects on personal experiences of the Spirit, Pentecostal, and Charismatic movements, the trinitarian context of ecumenical ministry, renaissance of theological reflection on the Trinity, and Salesian Spirituality. He references significant conferences, documents, and writers, including Anglican–Catholic, Lutheran–Catholic, and Evangelical–Catholic dialogues and Cardinal Kasper's work on harvesting the fruits of the ecumenical dialogue.

TOPICS

- Personal experience of the Holy Spirit
- Pentecostal and Charismatic Christians
- Pastoral Care
- Work of the Spirit in communities
- Human person as an image of the Trinity
- Role of the Spirit in ecumenism

CONCLUDING REFLECTIONS

"We laid some groundwork in this chapter for building a common ethical paradigm:"

- "The emphasis on the guidance of the Spirit.
- The human person as being in the image of the Trinity and thus made for relationships.
- The importance of spiritual gifts: certain Christians have the ability to understand moral issues in their complexity.
- A fourth foundational element is an emphasis on emotion and affect. The Spirit can speak to us through our feelings such as inner joy or sorrow. Modern sciences consider the physical and psychological connections of human emotions and reason. They are not separate. (Crossin, p. 14)"

DISCUSSION QUESTIONS/ REFLECTIONS

- What is your experience of the Holy Spirit?
- How do you see the human person as an image of the Trinity?
- How would you describe the interaction of head and heart?
- How do you see the Holy Spirit at work in the ecumenical movement today?

CLOSING PRAYER

Holy Spirit, help me in my discernment as an individual and as a member of a faith community. Guide us to seek the guidance of the Holy Spirit in all of our ministries, and especially in our ecumenical work, in Jesus' name. Amen

CHAPTER 2

Pastoral Ministry and Discernment

Opening Prayer: Lord, help us to do less talking and more listening. Help us listen to the Spirit speaking to us and not just listen to what we want to hear. May we discern the Spirit's guidance in all of our ecumenical endeavors. Amen

Brief Summary: Fr. Crossin says, "Two important elements for building a significant ecumenical moral paradigm are reflection on pastoral encounters and discernment of the voice of the Holy Spirit." (p. 15) Spiritual discernment is not just for those in ministry, but for all Christians. By virtue of our Baptism, all of us are called to follow the guidance of the Holy Spirit. The Spirit calls us to mission and into ecumenical adventures.

ACCOMPANIMENT AND DIALOGUE

- "Dialogue is more about listening than talking." (p. 15)

DISCERNMENT: INITIAL REFLECTIONS

- We walk, we serve

SALESIAN SPIRITUALITY

- St. Francis de Sales teaches us about patience, gentleness, humility, honesty, and more. All essential tools in dialoguing with our Christian brothers and sisters.

SALESIAN DISCERNMENT

- "DeSales reflections on discernment need to be approached in the context of regular personal prayer and reflection on the Scriptures." (p. 21)

COMMUNAL DISCERNMENT

- "Rather I will note two key elements of communal discernment. The first is detailed preparation." "The second key element is attention to the presentations of the members of the discerning groups." (p. 23) For detailed preparation for such a task force see Appendix. Most helpful.

PERSONAL REFLECTIONS

- Need time, places, and resources to gather.
- "This book is encouraging further discernment together by Christian communities on how to establish specific moral teaching." (Cf. six questions by Fr. Crossin on p. 24)

DISCUSSION QUESTIONS/REFLECTIONS

- What is your experience of discernment, as an individual and as a member of a faith community?
- St. Francis de Sales emphasizes the "little virtues" of humility, gentleness, patience. How do you think these virtues can facilitate our conversations with other Christian faith traditions?
- "Sometimes it is the least likely person who speaks God's word as we walk together and converse" (p.16). How can we be more open and alert to discern God's word when it may come from the "least likely person"?
- "What virtues and practices are needed to move discernment from being a practice for ministers and devout laity to being an essential dimension of moral life for all Christians?" (p.24)

CLOSING PRAYER

Lord, by the guidance of the Holy Spirit, help us to examine our own spiritual growth, listen to others, even the "least likely, "that we may discern how our spirituality can contribute to a communal, ecumenical conversation. In the name of Christ, we pray. Amen

CHAPTER 3

Biblical Ethics

OPENING PRAYER: Holy God, we acknowledge your presence in the Word. Thank you for giving us the Scriptures as a foundation for our Christian faith and moral decision making. Guide us in following your Word and living it daily.

BRIEF SUMMARY: In this chapter we learn about how Scripture has been used in moral interpretation, and the integration of biblical scholarship and ethics. Fr. Crossin suggests that the goal is "to develop an ecumenical ethical paradigm." (p. 31)

BIBLICAL ETHICS

- "Ecumenical ethics certainly will need to ground itself in prayer and biblical teaching." (p. 25)
- "Protestants, Orthodox, and Catholics now have a common biblical foundation for their personal moral reflection and communal life." (p. 26)
- "core elements for an ecumenical paradigm will come from the Scriptures." (p. 26)

HISTORICAL GLIMPSES

- "The common history of Christians dating back to the beginning focuses on the Scriptures." (p. 26)
- "Our history shows us that the moral theology of Roman Catholics did not depend much on the bible." (cf. footnote # 10, p. 28)
- "the Second Vatican Council encouraged Scripture study and a renewal of moral theology rooted in Scripture." (p. 28)

JEWISH BACKGROUND

- "One cannot really understand Jesus and the New Testament without the Jewish background." (p. 29)
- "Our work on an ecumenical ethic could include reference to Jewish scholars's interpretations of the Christian Bible " (p. 30)
- "We could likewise continue to pay attention to the views of Jewish ethicists as we address common moral issues." (p. 30)

THE INTEGRATION OF SCRIPTURE AND ETHICS

- "Our changing emphasis on our relationship with Jewish scholarship leads us into the work of Lucas Chan. He analyzed the work of both Catholic and Protestant scholars in the collaborative ecumenical spirit evident since the Second Vatican Council and the initiation of ecumenical dialogues." (p. 30–31)
- Chan: "while we seek unified Scriptural themes, we must also respect the diversity found in the Scriptures." (cf. footnote # 24, p. 31)

- Chan: "One's ethical framework is crucial to how biblical texts are used and interpreted." (cf. footnote # 25, p. 31) Crossin: "This is an important point for us to keep in mind as we develop an ecumenical ethical paradigm." (p. 31)

THE IMPORTANCE OF VIRTUE ETHICS

- "He (Chan) goes on to say that 'in terms of the narratives and the overall ends of the Scriptures themselves, we will see that virtue ethics is the most congruent and most able to bear the weight of interpretation." (cf. footnote # 32)

SOME RECENT DEVELOPMENTS

- Alain Thomassett: "Imagination is the mediation between the world of the text and the reader's appropriation." (cf. footnote #38, p. 33)
- Alain Thomassett: a fruitful encounter is needed between the proclamation of the Christian truth and the welcoming of human liberty. Crossin: "We can do this, using parables as Jesus did, because they activate the listener better than anything else." (cf. footnote # 39, p. 34)

CONCLUDING REFLECTIONS

- "In developing a paradigm for common Christian ethics, we will need to continue this collaboration and integration of the work of biblical and Christian ethicists." (p. 34)
- "Our need to relate gospel teaching to contemporary situations in various parts of the world will challenge our principles for interpretation." (p. 34)

DISCUSSION QUESTIONS/ REFLECTIONS

- In our reading and studying of the Bible, do we see its relevance to our lives?
- How do you utilize biblical texts in your own moral deliberations?
- What resources does your denominational tradition offer for our ecumenical learning of biblical scholarship and moral formation and discernment?
- Jesus told his parables to his apostles to teach them in a way they would understand. The stories related to their culture. What meaning do you get from the parables that help you to live your faith today? Think of one or two parables and how they relate to your life experiences.

CLOSING PRAYER

Gracious God, we thank you and praise you for the development, interpretation and scholarship of your Word and how, through those tools, you are helping us to learn and live the virtue of charity. We thank you in the name of Jesus, your son, Amen.

CHAPTER 4

Personal Relationships in a Relational Universe

OPENING PRAYER: Holy God, your revealed life as the Trinity is a model for relationships. Help us to make our relationships with each other the models of spiritual friendship and your healing love. Amen.

SUMMARY: "This chapter will concern itself with many aspects of our relationships—with one another in friendship, community, and ministry; with the natural world as understood by modern science; with our grounding in philosophy and theology; and with our history." (p.35)

PRELIMINARY OBSERVATIONS

- "Spiritual ecumenism is central to our ecumenical work." (p. 36)
- We need to know who we are and not identify ourselves in contrast to other churches.
- Positive changes since Vatican II: Scripture reading encouraged, new approaches to Catholic theology.

- The revival of the Catechumenate (a process of preparing adults and children of catechetical age for full initiation into the Catholic Church)
- Spiritualities such as Franciscan and Salesian gaining ground and promoting dialogue.
- "Our understanding of God, of the mystery of the Holy Trinity is limited. The call is to have the humility to acknowledge the limits of rational models." (p. 37)

ECUMENICAL FRIENDSHIPS

- In the context of prayer: "Ecumenically minded people often pray for the guidance of the Spirit in their discussions and in their ministry together." (p. 38)
- "Friends are a gift from God." (p. 38)
- Conversations: "A spiritual friend is one with whom we can discuss most aspects of life, including our spiritual journey." (p. 38)

RELATIONALITY IN OUR WORLD

- "The ongoing task of ecumenical ethics will be to integrate the scientific data into the best ethical thinking." (p. 40) "My contention is that an ecumenical ethics will need to consider that humans are relational beings in a relational universe as part of the foundations for its work." (p. 41)

SCIENCE AND RELIGION

- Faith and science do not contradict each other—they are a unity. However, this fact has not yet gained acceptance in the Christian community.
- "Our contention in this volume [is] that prayer and contemplation are part of building an ecumenical moral paradigm that deals with the total reality of the universe." (p. 42)

THEOLOGY AND RELATIONALITY: THE CONTEMPORARY CONTEXT

- The bible stresses community and relationships. Our culture stresses "the freedom to make one's own moral code." (p. 45)

PHILOSOPHICAL AND THEOLOGICAL REFLECTIONS ON RELATIONALITY

- This isolation fosters loneliness. "The epidemic of loneliness in the culture seems related to this downplaying of the importance of in-person relationships." (p. 46)

REFLECTIONS

- "In formal and informal ecumenical dialogues and in ecumenical friendships, in the fact that God is creating a relational universe, in philosophy and in theology, and in prayer and contemplation: I am arguing that relationality is a most important component of an ecumenical ethical paradigm." (p. 48)

Personal Relationships in a Relational Universe

DISCUSSION QUESTIONS/REFLECTIONS

- Do you have friends in a denomination not your own? Do you have a spiritual friend, one with whom you can discuss your spiritual journey?
- Where do you see isolation and loneliness in our culture, in our lives, in your own life?
- Reflect on how friendship, community, openness to differences, active listening could bridge the isolation of our culture and advance our ecumenical witness.
- What do you think St. Francis de Sales would advise?

CLOSING PRAYER

Lord, the only true freedom is found in our relationship with you. As the Holy Trinity sets the model for a community of love, guide us to live that love with our families, our neighbors, with different faith communities, the poor, and the marginalized. In the name of Jesus, Amen.

CHAPTER 5

Ecumenical Foundations / Dialogues

OPENING PRAYER: Holy Spirit, help us bring people together. Help us to move toward the future Fr. Crossin and his colleagues envisioned. Help us not to be afraid to discuss and pray about difficult issues and tensions. Help us to be open, honest, and receptive. We ask this in the name of Jesus Christ, our Lord. Amen.

SUMMARY: "Though the Spirit has been active since the beginning in the ecumenical movement, a focus on the Holy Spirit is a recent phenomenon in the Movement." (p. 49) Fr. Crossin describes the progress in several ecumenical documents and conferences, referencing Vatican II documents especially "The Decree on Ecumenism," 1964.

ECUMENICAL FOUNDATIONS/DIALOGUES

- "The work of Christian Unity is the work of the Holy Spirit. The past, present and future guidance of the Spirit grounds my optimism about the ecumenical movement. Current progress confirms this optimism." (p. 49)

- "Pope John XXIII's calling of the Second Vatican Council set in motion a host of processes"in ecumenical relations. (p. 49)
- Father Peter Hocken: "we need to re-think the distinguishing features between what is essentially Catholic and what we see as essentially Protestant." (cf. footnote #4, p. 50)

TODAY'S CONTEXT

- "For the Christian Churches in the United States in general, membership and attendance have continued to decline. In the same timeframe the ecumenical dialogues themselves hit harder issues—considered unresolvable by some authors—including the divergences on certain ethical issues." (p. 50)
- The pedophilia crisis offered us lessons in humility and self-examination but also the Spirit has given us the gifts to look outward and build stronger communities.
- "I believe that the Spirit has been at work while we have been self-preoccupied. The solutions are already present waiting to be acknowledged and implemented together" (p. 51)

THE JOINT DECLARATION ON THE DOCTRINE OF JUSTIFICATION (1999)

- "Immediately after the Second Vatican Council official dialogues between the Lutherans and the Catholics began in many countries. The International Dialogue is sponsored by the Lutheran World Federation and the Pontifical Council for Promoting Christian Unity. The process took over thirty years and involved many leading scholars. Justification was the key theological issue at the time of the Reformation." (p.52)

- "A crucial point is that God takes the initiative. Ecumenical convergences are the work of the Spirit and not just our own." (p.52)
- Fr. John goes on to quote some key paragraphs of the document. Well worth reading. A historical and groundbreaking document!

POPE FRANCIS' VIEW OF TENSIONS

- "Pope Francis's thinking allows for polarities that are in tension within the church. While some may be resolved, others continue to exist." (cf. footnote # 18, citation from *The Mind of Pope Francis* by Massimo Borghesi)
- "Pope Francis' thinking on oppositions helps us to realize that the oppositions can be the work of the Spirit in our midst, calling us to renew our thinking and feeling." (p. 55)

RECEPTIVE ECUMENISM

- "Receptive ecumenism is one of the major developments in the ecumenical movement in the last three decades. The dialogues that began after the Second Vatican Council no longer always discuss differences in their theological positions on church, sacraments, and so forth, but now might explore what the Spirit has given to one partner which can be adopted with benefit by the other." (p. 56)
- This method focuses on learning from dialogue partners rather than teaching them.

WALKING TOGETHER ON THE WAY

- "The Commission also asks what each tradition can learn from the inheritance of the other, and how far each tradition needs to undergo conversion, renewal and reform. This requires humility and patience." (*WTW,* no. 152, p. 58)
- "Catholics and Anglicans must give attention to what the Spirit may be saying in the other tradition before arriving at a definitive conclusion for their own tradition." (*WTW,* no.153, p. 58)

DECLARATION ON THE WAY

- Fr. Crossin modestly states, "I was gratified to have had a small part in putting together the 2015 *Declaration on the Way: Church, Ministry, and Eucharist* whish summarizes the work of Lutherans and Catholics in many countries." (p. 59) The document includes "thirty-two Agreed Statements, fifteen Remaining Differences, and Reconciling Considerations, and ten suggestions for local and regional collaboration." (p. 59)

COMMUNION IN GROWTH: THE FINNISH LUTHERAN-CATHOLIC DIALOGUE

- This report "has been able to say more than previous dialogues." (no. 367, cf. footnote # 30, p. 60)
- "One key point where the Finnish Lutheran-Catholic Dialogue agreed is that baptism and Eucharist are the major sacraments. The context for this consideration is the new relationship humanity and all creation have in Christ. Christians participate in this new relationship through baptism." (p. 61)

PERSONAL REFLECTIONS—LEADERSHIP FOR ECUMENICAL PROGRESS

- "The Holy Spirit has been guiding the churches over the years as we move carefully toward our goal of Christian unity. The recent documents cited above indicate to me that unity might be closer than we think." (p. 61)
- God is calling us to go deeper in 'spiritual ecumenism' and be attentive to the guidance of the Spirit as we come closer to our goal of unity. Prayerful discernment is the priority." (p. 61)
- "I believe that the Holy Spirit will give us the leaders we need as we move toward Christian unity." (p. 62)

DISCUSSION QUESTIONS/ REFLECTIONS

- I must make my own comment about this chapter. I am so encouraged by the hope and vision of Fr. John—a hope and vision much needed in our churches and in our world!
- What does religious identity mean to me?
- Can I let go and follow the Holy Spirit?
- What is non-negotiable or personal to me?
- Do I have ecumenical friends?[1]

CLOSING PRAYER

Fr. Crossin and St. Francis de Sales both say (paraphrased): Look to God, follow the Holy Spirit. Unity is in process. Keep moving forward. Listen and trust. Amen.

---

1. Last four questions taken from Fr. John Crossin, CMAX TV, videos on the book.

CHAPTER 6

Moral Systems

OPENING PRAYER: O God, you alone are holy. Help us to adapt, change, and discern amid changing moral systems and paradigms. Help us to open our hearts to the love, mercy, and peace of Jesus Christ and to be your holy people. Amen.

SUMMARY: "In this chapter, we give an overview of the meaning of paradigm and discuss the dominant Catholic paradigm, natural law . . . the love, mercy, and peace of Jesus Christ are foundational to Christian thinking." (p. 64)

MORAL PARADIGMS

- Thomas Khun in his *Structure of Scientific Revolutions* "asserted that a paradigm 'is declared invalid only if an alternative candidate is available to take its place.'" (cf. footnote # 7, p. 65)

CATHOLIC THINKING ON NATURAL LAW

- "Natural Law" has been dominant in Catholic thinking, for example, *Human Vitae*, 1968, opposing artificial contraception.

- "A revolution/crisis [in natural law application] has begun and continues." (p. 65)
- "There has been some interest in Natural Law as a foundational paradigm for Protestants circles." (p. 65)
- Fr. Crossin references German theologian Eberhard Schokenhoff:
- "Schokenhoff believes that the world religions of the major ethical traditions should enter dialogue and be open to learning from one another." (cf. footnote # 14, p. 67)

THEOLOGICAL PARADIGMS

- Mark Massa: "Thus talking about natural law is messy and chaotic, and the development of human models of it are, by definition, non–linear because reality is always more complex than any model we can construct to explain it." (cf. footnote # 23, p. 69)
- "The ecumenical emphasis on unity and justice, on the necessity of a wholistic dialogue that is interdisciplinary, and on the fact that reality is complex and not easily captured by human models speaks to the process and the limits of constructing paradigm for ecumenical ethics." (p. 69)
- "I leave Massa's book thinking that the debate and discussion over natural law will be continuing. I believe that our search for a moral paradigm might best first concern itself with biblical teaching." (p. 70)
- "I would add that biblically nourished spiritual growth will be necessary as Christians work together toward consensus on ethics." (p. 71)

PERSONAL REFLECTIONS ON A PARADIGM

- "The debate and discussion over natural law will be continuing. I believe that our search for a moral paradigm might best first concern itself with biblical teaching." (p. 70)
- "Prayer with and study of the biblical witness is certainly a common emphasis among Protestants, Anglicans, Orthodox and Catholics today." (p. 70)
- "I would add that biblically nourished spiritual growth will be necessary as Christians work together toward consensus on ethics." (p. 71)

JESUS OUR SAVIOR AND EXEMPLAR

- "The core elements common to all ecumenical moral paradigms will be drawn from Scripture. Thus, we now turn to a few considerations of Jesus as the center of our moral reflection." (p. 71)
- "Our commitment to a relationship with Jesus Christ is the key foundation for an ecumenical ethic. Jesus is the paradigmatic person." (p. 71)
- Salesian spirituality is woven throughout Fr. Crossin's life, ministry, teaching, preaching, and his writings, as an Oblate priest. He refers to our creation in God's image, the centrality of love, freedom, and the virtues. "We only attain our full humanity in Christ." (p. 72)

THE IMPORTANCE OF MERCY

- Pope Francis, in his papacy and writings, emphasizes mercy and loving. Mercy was the theme of the Jubilee Year.

- "Our common moral paradigm(s) will focus on the virtue of love manifested in Jesus. Individual virtues such as humility, patience, gentleness, and perseverance are natural virtues that can be animated by love." (p. 74)
- "I believe that the dialogue over a common ethical paradigm will involve a sharing of these gifts. The dialogue partners will be called to a receptive ecumenism—receiving the Spirit's gifts from others and sharing our Spirit-endowed gifts with them. In this way an ecumenical paradigm will emerge." (p. 74)

DISCUSSION QUESTIONS/REFLECTIONS

- What are the challenges that Fr. Crossin gives us in order to create a "common moral paradigm?"
- What are some of the gifts and virtues we need to live a moral life?
- Do we feel empowered and honest enough to discuss these questions with our friends, family, neighbors, and Christians from faith traditions not our own?
- Does this book so far (chapter 6) motivate us to move toward Fr. Crossin's future? If so, what are some steps we can take?

CLOSING PRAYER

Lord, the model of Jesus' life and message is clear, but not always easy to apply in our time and place. Lord, help us to listen, accept, trust so that we can move toward being one in Christ. Amen.

CHAPTER 7

Virtue Ethics Today

OPENING PRAYER: Loving God, thank you for the example of St. Francis de Sales, who reminds us that the "little virtues" of peace, patience, kindness, gentleness, love, humility are the ones most frequently needed in our daily lives. Through your Spirit, help us to live them every day, that we might grow in goodness and love of neighbor. In Jesus' name we pray. Amen

SUMMARY: This chapter describes the key elements of virtue ethics, critiques of virtue ethics, love and moral development.

KEY ELEMENTS OF A VIRTUE ETHIC

- "It is usually not the individual but the faithful community together that grows in moral wisdom. This points to the need for Christian traditions to come together to discuss moral paradigms. This book is a prelude to such a discussion, not a replacement for it." (p. 77)
- "Spiritual practices shape the character of the person." (p. 78)

CRITIQUES OF VIRTUE ETHICS

- "One critique is that with the burgeoning of Virtue Ethics, the reader needs to be clear about an individual author's definition of terms and conception of virtue." (p. 78)
- "A second critique has to do with perfectionism." The seeker of virtues might focus on human effort and not the grace that enables the person to live a virtuous life." (p. 79)
- "Friendship is the key to spiritual growth. This includes friendship with self, friendship with others, and friendship with God" (cf, footnote #18)
- Faith journey is complicated and often not clear. "Life is complex, and the Spirit's guidance can often seem unclear." (p. 79)

LOVE AS THE CENTRAL VIRTUE

- The primary virtue for St. Francis de Sales is love. "The goal is a life totally dedicated to the love of God by seeking to turn everything to the good." (p. 81)
- Fr. Crossin describes the four stages of love that St. Francis de Sales describes in his Treatise on the Love of God. These four stages are described on p. 82. (cf. footnotes # 28, 29 and 30)

BIBLICAL REFLECTIONS ON COSTLY LOVE

- John Armstrong's book Costly Love, asserts "Costly love is God's will for us." Armstrong believes that our basic problems are not doctrinal but relational." (p. 83)

DEVELOPMENTAL PSYCHOLOGY

- "Lawrence Kohlberg (1927–87) made the psychology of moral development an important sub-field within psychology with his studies of justice reasoning of young people in the United States and in other countries as well. Kohlberg contended that the stages of moral development were universal in scope." (cf. footnote # 40, p. 84–85)

LAW'S VIRTUES

- "Respect for law and development of virtues are concomitant at each stage of moral development with law dominant in earlier life and virtue later." (p. 86)
- "Our relationships with others continue to have impact on our moral and spiritual growth throughout life." (p. 86)

CONCLUDING REFLECTIONS

- "As we see in the ancient church and the Middle Ages, obedience to the law and the virtuous life are not opposed but complementary. I suggest that the Ten Commandments provide boundaries for moral behavior." (p. 88)
- "Christian ethics is deeply rooted in practices of doing good both individually and as a member of a community of faith." "Most change is slow. God's grace operates within us and our communities over time." (p. 88)

DISCUSSION QUESTIONS/REFLECTIONS

- How do you make moral decisions?

- Do you consider doctrine and relationships?
- How do you deal with change?[2]
- How might you as an individual and your faith community pray about and then deepen your practices of doing good?

CLOSING PRAYER

Lord, help us to treat others with dignity, love and compassion. Help us to be gentle as we work through our differences and change. Inspire us to work together toward deeper moral practices through the guidance of the Spirit. In Jesus's name, we pray. Amen.

---

2. Taken from Fr. Crossin's video, Talk 3, CMAX TV.

CHAPTER 8

Moral Acts and the Promise of Peacebuilding

OPENING PRAYER: Lord, we are a country and a world needing peace! Why do we get caught up in division, violence, turmoil, and anger? How can we build peace? How can we transform our lives? Lord, you are the Way: moral decision making, tolerance, moral acts, virtues, participating in a community of love and justice. These are some of the tools we need to follow you. Help us on our journey of faith! We ask this in your name, Jesus, Amen.

SUMMARY: THIS CHAPTER ADDRESSES:

- "Dimensions of the moral act;
- the importance of peacebuilding both in the world and between/within Christian churches
- three virtues—inner peace, honesty, and love—that are appropriate to peace building;
- and what peacebuilding might say to us about ecumenical ethics."

- "Neurobiology's data on how humans learn and how the brain works might nuance our traditional analysis of the moral act." (p. 89)

THE CONTRIBUTION OF NEUROETHICS

- "I would agree that Christians need to take a critical attitude toward the data and the claims of scientists."
- "Their infield critique can provide helpful guidance as to how the scientific information might fit in with theological reflection."
- Salzman and Lawler: "They proceed to consider the relationship of neurotheology to 'attention, emotion, free will and experience.'" (cf. footnote # 4, and p. 89)
- "Moral theology today seems to be moving from highly ordered planning (left brain dominant) to more disorderly/creative personal experiences (right brain "dominant)." (p. 91)
- "It is God's grace that liberates our bound wills." (cf. footnote # 10)
- Fr. Crossin was a Salesian optimist and gave "more emphasis to grace." (p. 91)

THE MORAL ACT

- "we should consider the importance of moral law and incorporate it into our virtue paradigm as part of human moral development." (p. 92)
- "The model—drawing on the Scriptures and dating back to the Middle Ages—speaks of the object, the circumstances, and the intention of the act." (p. 92)

Moral Acts and the Promise of Peacebuilding

- "The object and circumstances of the moral act were considered in detail in Catholic moral theological debate in the decades after the Second Vatican Council. "More recently, attention has focused on reason itself." (cf. footnote # 14, p. 93)
- Christina McRorie notes that, "Catholic moral theology is reevaluating its long-standing confidence in human reason, most recently in light of a growing awareness of the deleterious effects of social sin." (cf. footnote # 16)
- "All the factors just mentioned—influences on reasoning, the act and it circumstances, factors influencing intention—deserve critical and deep study." Any ecumenical group working on moral discernment will need to take a careful look at these factors and act with 'Epistemic Humility.'" (p. 94)

BAPTIZED INTO A COMMUNITY

- "We are baptized into a community of belief. Interestingly, Christians, despite our differences, tend to recognize one another's baptism. At a basic spiritual level, we are joined to one another." (p. 95)
- "Communities can be places where persons are valued and personal gifts can flourish, or they can be places where prejudices and negative actions decrease freedom and limit human possibilities." (p. 96)

PEACE OF HEART

- "The presence and proclamation of the gospel of Jesus Christ includes inner peace and peace building." (p. 96)
- "The reader is aware that the Spirit is in the community and will remain with the community forever, but the community

- must reach beyond its own borders to continue the mission of Jesus." (cf. footnote # 27)
- "Peacefulness often flows out of a life of prayer where we take as much time listening to what God might be saying to us as we take offering petitions for those in need." (cf. footnote # 29)
- "A 'Gentle Peace' can be both in our hearts and in our midst." (p. 97)

PEACEBUILDING

- "The ecumenical movement over the last century has been a successful international effort in building peace rather than continuing religious strife and divisions." (p. 97)
- "Peacebuilding is an ongoing process not only a necessity in crisis. Our goal would be to build relationships that prevent differences from coming to violence. An example of this is the Interfaith Council of Metropolitan Washington, D.C." (p. 99)

SPIRITUAL DIMENSIONS OF PEACEBUILDING

- Myles Werntz writing about Howard Thurman: "A non-violent approach to racism and violence is possible, Thurman believed, only because of a transformative encounter with God In the mystical encounter of prayer, not only do people transcend the doctrinal particularities which divide Christians in prayer people are driven to confront the core issue of violence—the self-righteous and egoistic self." (cf. footnote # 37)
- "My own observations, in the practice of spiritual direction, is that moving closer to God's love/mercy in meditation and contemplation—or more precisely, letting God move closer

to us—is a long-term endeavor empowered by the Spirit." (cf. footnote # 39)

THE IMPORTANCE OF HONESTY

- "A virtue related to humility, honesty with ourselves and others, is not much valued in public discourse in the United States these days but it is absolutely essential for peacebuilding." (p. 100)
- "Dishonest history can have deleterious effects for coming generations. On the one hand, public processes of engaging the truth, difficult as that may be, can help short-circuit generations of dishonesty as we see in the various Truth and Reconciliation efforts throughout the world." (p. 102)

LOVE OUR NEIGHBOR AND OUR ENEMY

- "As we mentioned earlier, the law (the commandment) provides a boundary. It alerts us that we may be heading off course. At times we need such warnings. But what we are seeking more deeply is love of neighbor and even of enemies without recriminations." (p. 102)

PASTORAL PREPARATIONS

- "The ongoing process of peacebuilding calls for a variety of virtues such as hope, patience, courage, humility, and inner peace to name just a few." (p. 103)

PERSONAL REFLECTIONS EMBODYING VIRTUES

- "Peacebuilding calls for an ongoing life of prayer, for the practice of virtues, and for practical preparation. It also calls for personal discernment." (p. 104)
- "'What is God calling me to do?' If we have inner peace and joy in our times of prayer and discernment, we have one of the classic signs that the Holy Spirit is guiding us. This gives us some, but not absolute, confidence in our discernment." (p. 104)
- "Part of my purpose in writing is to encourage dialogue, collaboration, and ecumenical ethical paradigm-building that, with the guidance of the Spirit, can bring Christians together." (p. 104)

DISCUSSION QUESTIONS/REFLECTIONS

- Do you participate in a faith community? If yes, how does it support you?
- What virtues are highlighted in this chapter? Why?
- Can you name the gifts God has given you?
- How is God calling you to use them? Spiritual Direction can help you discern the answer to this question.
- Can you explain to yourself and others how reason and emotion help you to determine moral acts?
- When we come to Christian Unity will you be ready?

CLOSING PRAYER

Dear loving God, thank you for the gifts you have given me. Help me to discern how you want me to use them. Give me the courage to trust that the Holy Spirit will help me to facilitate peacebuilding in whatever circumstances I find myself. I ask this in the name of Jesus Christ, our Lord, Amen.

CHAPTER 9

Ecumenical Reflections on Moral Discernment

OPENING PRAYER: Lord Jesus, Help us in our moral discernment. Help us to reflect on the Scriptures, the teachings and doctrine of the Church, our experiences, our faith tradition and give us the courage to share our experiences and openly listen to the sharing of others. We ask all this in your name, Jesus. Amen.

SUMMARY

- "This chapter will develop our reflections on moral discernment in the churches. These reflections will include two of the documents of the Faith and Order Commission of the World Council of Churches that appeared in recent months." (cf. footnote # 1) These are volume 1 *Churches and Moral Discernment Learning from Traditions,* and volume 2 *Churches and Moral Discernment Learning from History.* (cf. footnote # 2) "I will conclude with a proposal that some of the churches that have endorsed *JDDJ* [*Joint Declaration on the Doctrine of Justification*] establish a Working Group to develop an *Ecumenical Ethical Paradigm.*" (p. 105)

- "The *Moral Discernment in the Churches* text begins by offering four reasons, which we must keep in mind, why moral consensus is so difficult to attain." (p. 106) See these four reasons on p. 106.

REFLECTIONS

- "In reflecting on these two sections of Causative Factors, we learn that it is important for dialogue partners to get to know one another personally. Sessions might include (1) sharing of one's personal experience of the question being discussed or (2) her/his feelings about the issue under discussion or (3) or any stereotypes that he/she knows they bring to such a discussion." (p. 107)
- "The fact is that, not without considerable effort on the part of the dialogue partners and with the guidance of the Spirit, we have come to agreements on many matters and can do so on moral issues as well." (p. 107)
- "My own suggestion is structured dialogue. I believe that a task force with expertise in various moral sources and drawing expert members from the world church, might explore issues raised in this report [*Moral Discernment in the Churches*]and the others that follow it." (p. 108)

CHURCHES AND MORAL DISCERNMENT. VOL 1: LEARNING FROM TRADITIONS

- "This 2021 document presents essays on how moral decisions are made in fourteen Christian traditions—authored by their own experts. It is meant to be informative and 'enable conversation and mutual listening' and giving an account of sources of authority and ecclesial structures involved in moral discernment." (cf. footnote # 11, p. 108)

- "[W]e will focus further comments on those Christian traditions that have formally endorsed the *JDDJ*. This gives them a common 'platform' on which to build. (cf. footnote # 13) Our emphasis will be primarily on issues relating to moral thinking and not on ecclesiology." (p. 109)

SCRIPTURE, TRADITION, AND REASON

- Jeremy Worthen notes that "Anglicans have often identified scripture, tradition, and reason as the three primary sources for moral authority " (cf. footnote # 14, p. 109)
- Morgan Logan wrote that in Methodism, "Wesley also recognized the significance of human experience, especially Christian religious experience in theological discernment.'" (p. 109)
- Rebecca Todd Peters notes that "a Reformed theological perspective holds that human understandings and interpretations of the gospel do change and grow as the human community changes and grows." (cf. footnote # 16, p. 110)
- Crossin: "I note here a coherence in recognizing the fundamental sources of moral theology with Scripture being at the center. I would mention that, in line with our common emphasis on spiritual ecumenism, our understanding of the inspired Scriptures can always go deeper." (p. 110)

SYNODALITY

- Jeremy Worthen "mentions that Authority has been a major topic in Anglican –Catholic dialogue. He goes on to speak of 'Synodality' and its development in the Anglican tradition since the nineteenth century. The role of the laity in these synods has increased over the years since then." (cf. footnote # 19, p. 110)

- Joseph Romelt in an essay explains magisterium in the Catholic Church but notes "there has never been a solemn dogmatic declaration on an ethical topic." (cf. footnote # 20, p. 110)
- "The Catholic church under Pope Francis has encouraged Synodality and has encouraged surveys of laity before recent synods." (p. 110)
- "Each of the communities, and the Lutherans also as I have personally experienced, value the thinking of the members of the communities. Forms of Synodality should encourage moral discernment that listens for the voice of the Spirit speaking through the members of the community." (p. 111)

THE ROLE OF BISHOPS AND CLERGY

- Methodist bishops have no authoritative voice but they do sit in council and assign clergy. (p. 111)
- Presbyterians emphasize basic equality of clergy and laity. (p. 111)
- "The Catholic Church is well known for its Magisterium of the Pope and the bishops." (p. 112)
- For Lutheran churches implementation of moral norms resides with the conscientious individual. (cf. footnote # 26, p. 112)

BINDING FORCE OF CHURCH TEACHING

- Anglicans: "official moral teaching should be as far as possible commendatory rather than prescriptive or binding." (cf. footnote # 27, p. 112)
- Lutheran Augsburg Confession "states that the bishop should be preaching to convince not coerce." (cf. footnote # 28, p. 112)

- "These stances contrast with Catholics who offer arguments that they hope are persuasive in authoritative documents but also expect that church teaching will be followed." (p. 112)
- Presbyterian: "Because members of the Presbyterian tradition believe that the Holy Spirit works through elected leaders to help illuminate the truth of the gospel for our times, the authority represented in these councils and their statement is voluntarily accepted as the wisdom or the church." (cf. footnote # 29, p. 112)

INFORMED MORAL JUDGMENT

- "I would note here that regarding the topics of bishops and clergy, authority and informed moral judgment, a both/and approach can be helpful." (p. 113)
- The conscientious Christian must act as appropriate to the situation." (p. 113)

PENULTIMATE

- "We cannot decide in advance what is more or what is less [as opposed to either/or]. It depends on context, which might also change." (p. 113)
- "Bonhoeffer and Peters both refer to what we have called 'relative' certainty." (p. 114)

A COMMON MORAL THEOLOGY

- "The five Christian communities whose scholars' essays we have excerpted above seem to have convergence on more than justification. *All in practice have the inspired Scriptures* at the center and emphasis on tradition, reason, and experience as they judge appropriate." (p. 114)

- "While the Catholic Church seems to be sorting out how synods will work in practice, synods and their cognates are standard for the signatories of the *JDDJ*." (cf. footnote # 35, p. 114)

- Fr. Crossin wondered if, at national denominational meetings, his colleagues would be influenced by church politics. "If so, I wonder how these conversations would relate to discerning God's will. And I also wonder about the influence of secular cultures. In developing a paradigm for moral decision in a world church, how will we account for the influence of cultures and their benign and questionable influences?" (p. 115)

- "Lay participation is most important as those who have the charism of leadership/authority seek God's will for the community." (cf. footnote # 37. p. 115)

- If Individuals or a group has been called by the Spirit, has the charism of authority, and has listened to the community in discerning the guidance of the Spirit I would think that their teaching should be presumed correct and that, while conscientious dissent is possible, it should be highly informed by consultation, study, prayer, and discernment like that of those who have received the charism." (p. 116)

- "Here we should note that Christian moral decision–making has an impact on members of the community who are not Christians, and that impact must be taken into consideration out of love for our neighbor." (p. 116)

CHURCHES AND MORAL DISCERNMENT, VOL. 2, LEARNING FROM HISTORY

- "The second text, also released in 2021, considers changes in moral teaching over the centuries. Nineteen scholars were asked to provide essays. These essays deal with usury (3), slavery (3), church–state–society (4), war and non–violence (3), women in liturgy (1), marriage (3) and suicide (2)." (p. 116)

- Myriam Wijlens and Vladimir Somali "note that differences on moral questions can become a 'threat to an existing unity or prevent the restoration of Christian unity.'" (cf. footnote # 41, p. 116)

- "These divisions can impede unity. They also can be an impediment to spreading the gospel message." (p. 116)

- Simone Senn: "Insights from the Study Process.""These include the fact that a new understanding of the phenomenon [of evolving moral stances over time] led to a change in moral teaching A second reason for change is the churches' moral failures A third reason for change has been the realization that the church is not upholding the dignity of the human person including 'the call of service to vulnerable people.'" (p. 117)

FURTHER ECUMENICAL RESOURCES

- "The three Faith and Order documents discussed above provide a wealth of ecumenical resources for deeper dialogue on moral issues. They will be most helpful in working with divisions that already exist. I should mention that the goal of this volume is to begin to develop a forward–looking moral paradigm that representatives of Christian churches can use as a framework for evaluating new moral issues or revisiting old ones." (p. 118)

- Fr. Crossin in the rest of this section highlights three recent sources pertinent to this discussion.

CONCERNING DIVISIVE ISSUES

- In this section, Fr. Crossin commends the recent book *Discerning Ethics: Diverse Christian Responses to Divisive Moral Issues* (Hak Joon Lee and Tim Dearborn, eds,) which is devoted to "sixteen controversial issues in social ethics each of which is discussed at some length." (p. 119)

- Hak Joon Lee, in his introduction wrote: "Even while we believe in one God, serve one Lord, pray in the one Spirit, and read one book, we are often radically divergent in our understanding of God's will on particular social issues." He continues to write that preachers "do not want to upset people, but the outcome is that many Christians are more influenced by secular ideologies than they are by the corporate spiritual formation by their congregation." (cf. footnote # 52, pp. 119–20)

- Hak Joon Lee: "Every ethical decision should be pursued prayerfully and communally in the love of God and others, and be open to mutual testing, correction, affirmation, and challenge from brothers and sisters in Christ " (cf. footnote # 54, p.1 20)

- Tim Dearborn: "Likewise, in our ethical positions, we are called to make sure that we are not bowing our knee to any political party, social ideology, national loyalty, or personal self-interest." (cf. footnote # 56, p. 120)

DEVELOPMENT OF DOCTRINE

- Fr. Crossin discusses Jesuit Historian John W. O'Malley, author of *When Bishops Meet: An Essay Comparing Trent, Vatican I and Vatican II*. "His scholarly work provides additional understanding that moral teaching can and does change over time." (p. 121)

- "O'Malley goes on to note that by the beginning of the Second Vatican Council theologians and bishops took change for granted. 'Their only questions were about how to explain it, about how far it could legitimately go, and what the criteria were for making changes.'" (cf. footnote # 59, p. 121)
- "Our examination of the history of the Second Vatican Council on development and our concise summary of the teaching of Cardinal Newman on doctrinal development remind us that change is part of the spiritual journey of the churches as they come together." (cf. footnote # 65)

CROSSIN'S MORAL PARADIGM PROPOSAL

- *"I am proposing that some of the signatories of JDDJ sponsor a Working Group that seeks to construct a common moral paradigm.* This suggestion is a move forward from 'this is how our Christian tradition makes moral decisions' to 'these are the gift(s) of the Spirit that we have to contribute to a common moral framework.' It is time to move into the future and not be paralyzed by some current disagreements." (p. 123)
- Fr. Crossin's paradigm is to be built on ten pillars which can be found in the Introduction, in the chapters, and in the appendix. These pillars "would be the task of the Working Group."
- There would be changes/nuances in moral teaching and "change in methods of authoritative approval." (p. 123)
- "We are in the context of a world church. The presuppositions of the European/North American theologies cannot be taken for granted. Thus, in this volume I have proposed spiritual, pastoral, biblical and relational foundations and in general have avoided presupposing the Greek philosophy which is not a common denominator in a world church." (p. 123)
- "A second change in context is that Christian ethics has itself has become more complex. There is a need for individuals to

engage in dialogue who have expertise in many fields—such as psychology, neurobiology, scripture, and ecclesiology—that we have mentioned in this volume." (p. 124)
- On p.124, Fr. Crossin has additional recommendations for the Working Group. Be sure to take note of them.

DISCUSSIONS/REFLECTIONS

- Can you think of some ideologies and cultural influences that might have been of some concern for Fr. Crossin, or that concern you?
- What different experiences and gifts do clergy and laity bring to the ecumenical dialogue?
- What are some of the positive and negative issues that surface in Christian history and in your tradition?
- Why and how has Christian ethics become more complex?
- Why and how has moral teaching changed and evolved over time?
- There have now been two recent synods in the Catholic church. Were you part of the preparation process and/or participation in the synod? What was your experience?

CLOSING PRAYER

Dear Lord, our world today is so diverse and complex and yet You call us to love, respect and honor all creation and all of your people. It is not always easy to discern the right and moral way to live but we know that if we open up our hearts to your grace and wisdom, we will honor you and your people. Lead us God! We ask all this in the name of your son, Jesus Christ, Amen.

CHAPTER 10

An Ecumenical Paradigm for Moral Teaching

OPENING PRAYER: Lord Jesus, guide us as we move toward full communion. Help us to spread the gospel faithfully, coherently, and effectively that your name may be glorified by all people. We ask this in your holy name, Amen.

SUMMARY: A CONSTRUCTIVE PROPOSAL

- "In this chapter, we will present many of the significant elements in this ecumenical ethical paradigm: biblical teaching, fundamental sacraments, future orientation, the Faith and Order 'Tool' which can help dissonant voices come to a mutual understanding, the ten foundational elements, and some ways to look at issues—differentiated consensus, accepting tensions in the church, and dealing with a human tendency to universalize our personal experience. All these parts are part of the ongoing development of an ethical paradigm." (p. 125)

- Fr. Crossin refers his readers to the gospel account of the disciples meeting Jesus on the road to Emmaus. Read his

AN ECUMENICAL PARADIGM FOR MORAL TEACHING

- description of the similarities between their conversation and our ecumenical dialogues. (p. 125–26)
- "The New Testament contains a tension between what theologians call 'already' and 'not yet' the 'already' of the salvation that has come and the 'not yet' of completed salvation." (p. 126)
- Dennis Billy writes: "Jesus' message is spread primarily through the witness of saintly lives, of people who are thoroughly committed to following their Lord." (cf. footnote # 8, p. 127)

THE FUNDAMENTAL SACRAMENTS: BAPTISM AND EUCHARIST

- "The Finnish Lutheran–Catholic dialogue in its 2017 statement offered a detailed study of sacraments and agreed that baptism and Eucharist are the central sacraments in the Church." (p. 127)
- "The dialogue addressed remaining issues and stated that 'a joint declaration on the Church, Eucharist, and Ministry is needed as the next step.' (no. 367). I believe this would be a momentous step." (p. 127)
- "The Holy Spirit will gift us with deeper insight into our moral teachings through the Word, sacrament, gathered community, and its presider as we pray together at the Eucharist/Lord's Supper. (cf. footnote # 10) Our prayer together can both flow from and lead to deeper contemplation." (p.128)

PRELIMINARIES

- "Drawing on my remarks in chapter 9, I would stress: that it is important for dialogue members who are working on such a paradigm to get to know one another; that Scripture is central but tradition, reason, and experience also have an important role; that some common criteria for communal discernment are necessary; and that the charism of authority calls on leaders to make decisions toward unity in a timely fashion." (p. 128)

- "In seeking to build a moral paradigm we are listening for the 'tiny whispering sound' by which the Spirit guides us in ways we would never have expected. What God wills for us is the best! Our best attitude is one of gratitude to God." (p. 128)

- "A prime spiritual question we might be asking ourselves is: 'How can I turn this particular situation to the good? or 'How might I use the gifts God has given me to make this bad situation better (which is not to say perfect)?'" (p. 129)

- "What is of concern at this moment to the ecumenically minded Christian Churches is the already–existing difference on moral issues that are causing divisions within and between the churches." (p. 129)

MOVING TOWARDS CONSENSUS, FACILITATING DIALOGUE TO BUILD KOINOIA (CF. FOOTNOTE # 13)

- *Three important elements* in this document: "First, we should mention that we count very much on people's sincerity even though it does not mean we will agree on a given issue (no. 23)." (p. 130)

- "*Secondly,* the text defines the *conscience of the church* (nos. 24–26). The *conscience of the church* involves the whole community." (p. 130)

- "*Thirdly,* the fourth chapter offers 'A Tool to Understand Disagreement and Facilitate Dialogue to Build Koinoia.'" (p. 131). See a,b,c,d,e for detailed exposition and description of the "Tool," pages 131 and 132.

An Ecumenical Paradigm for Moral Teaching

REFLECTIONS

- *"Facilitating Dialogue* "sees a process rooted in Christian commitment, prayer, and discernment of the guidance of the Spirit. Its emphasis falls much more on norms than on virtues. Its focus is on moral contradictions in the present moment. It does not offer a systematic approach to engaging future issues—though it might be helpful in doing so." (p. 132)
- "*Facilitating Dialogue* also does not mention the assistance of a spiritual guide in discernment." (p. 132)
- "The 'Tool' just discussed is a most welcome addition which can help bring Christian communities closer together or even to agreement on controverted issues." (p. 133)

ELEMENTS FOR A MORAL PARADIGM—SERMON ON THE MOUNT

- "How can we be consistent with what Jesus taught? Our contemporary discussions can tend to focus on single moral issues as if they were independent from other issues. A paradigm reminds us of the interconnections of issues within Christian morality." (p. 133)
- "Another advantage in speaking in terms of paradigms is that paradigms can change gradually as new thinking is integrated with old but occasionally can change dramatically based on some central insight that affects all or most of the important moral questions." (p. 133)
- "The four major scriptural elements for any moral paradigm: *the Sermon on the Mount, the commandments to love God and neighbor, the Ten Commandments, and the works of Mercy (Matt 25:31–46)* cohere well with the word and example of

the earliest Christians and Christians down through the centuries to our own time." (cf. footnote # 16)

- Daniel Harrington, scripture scholar "has five main elements in his approach to the Sermon itself." (cf. footnote # 20, p. 134)

CATEGORIZING MORAL ISSUES

- "Christians agree completely on many moral issues. Further ecumenical considerations moving Christian communities toward moral consensus on divisive issues would include looking at them through different lenses." (p. 135)

A. Joint Declaration—Differentiated Consensus

- "Our common foundations are in Scripture. *JDDJ* affirms newer methods of discovering the meaning of Scripture such as the historical-critical method for the world behind the text and narrative criticism which considers both the author and the reader in front of the text." (cf. footnote # 22, p. 135)
- "The importance of the trinitarian foundation to the *JDDJ* and the work on ecumenical ethics should not be underestimated." (p. 135)
- "The Christian's active love is enabled by the Holy Spirit." (p. 136)

B. Polarities and Synodality

- "Full communion between Catholics and Protestants and Orthodox, our ecumenical vision, might include 80 percent of all Christians." (cf. footnote # 26). "This is well over a billion people. It would be naïve to think there will not be differences of opinion and tensions." (p. 136)
- "Pope Francis discussion of polarities, which draws from the work of Romano Guardini, speaks of contradictions which

can lead to divisions and tensions that can lead to new synthesizes." (p. 137)

- "One danger here is that groups will withdraw into circles or perceived safety and ignore the Spirit's guidance. Rather, one should emphasize the tensions within the church that force us to get out of ourselves and our worlds and encounter other Christians, learn from them, and become holy." (p. 137)

- "Synodality is essential to our ongoing dialogue about controverted moral issues." (p. 138)

C. Universalizing

- "There can be a tendency to generalize one's personal and communal experience or one's moral insight and say it should be applied to all Christians! All Christians is an exceptionally large number of people in today's world church. It seems to me that such human tendencies should be addressed at a local or regional level perhaps though the efforts of a local ecumenical synod." (p. 138—139)

AN EXPLORATORY WORK

- "This concluding chapter is as much exploratory as definitive. As with other parts of this text I am seeking to contribute to what I perceive will be an ongoing discussion of Christian ethics—even after churches come into full communion. Many moral issues and perspectives change over time." (p. 139)

- "Of particular interest, given the reflections above, is the impact of Virtue Ethics. Many Catholic, Protestant, and Orthodox ethicists embrace VE." (p. 139)

- David Cloutier and Anthony Ahrens: "The authors suggest social cognitive theory provides key insights into the mechanics of agents 'acting from character' and offers an

- empirical program that can further our understanding of moral disagreement." (p. 139)
- "The emphasis of SCT on both cognition and social context should satisfy many moralists." (cf. footnote # 33) "This model emphasizes an interaction between the person and the situation." (p. 140)
- "My intuition is that this development of a virtuous moral act could offer a way forward on some disagreements." (p. 140)
- "Saint Francis de Sales mentions that in the spiritual life we are always either backwards or forwards. There is always motion though sometimes it is subtle." (p. 140)

FINAL REFLECTION

- "My hope in writing is that we can begin to see more clearly the outlines of a moral paradigm that integrates both norms and virtues. We have many elements but not the total framework." (p. 141)
- "What I would suggest would be an international group of moralists that needs to address the question of (a) common moral paradigms and related issues. Christian ethics today is complicated and no one person has expertise in all its dimensions. Christian ethics today calls for a team. Works such as this book are beginnings not endings." (p. 141)
- "As I did earlier in this volume, I do take stances on some central issues. I list elements for a moral paradigm and believe that biblical teaching and especially the four major elements listed earlier in this chapter take center stage in an ecumenical ethics." (p. 141)

DISCUSSION QUESTIONS/ REFLECTIONS

- What are the moral tensions that your Christian community is addressing right now?
- Do we universalize our experiences? What are some concerns about doing that?
- Why do you think Fr. Crossin chose the gospel the "Road to Emmaus" as a comparison to ecumenical dialogue?
- Fr. Crossin quotes the "tiny whispering sound" that the prophet Elijah heard and recognized the voice of the Spirit. Do we hear those sounds? To whom should we turn in getting help to listen and understand these sounds?
- Why did Fr. Crossin write that his book is just a beginning not an ending? What did he envision for the future? How can you be a part of that vision, that future?

CLOSING PRAYER

Jesus, Son of God, nothing is impossible if it is your will! Guide us and help us to understand how, in our own space in the world, we can contribute to the efforts to create Christian unity among our sisters and brothers. Show us the way and help us to be open to answering your call! We ask this in your name. Amen.

Biographical History

FR. JOHN CROSSIN, OSFS (1947—2023)

Fr. John Crossin was born in Philadelphia in 1947, the oldest of four children. He attended St. Matthew's parish grammar school. He attended Father Judge High School. After graduation in 1965, he joined the Oblates of St. Francis de Sales. He was ordained into the priesthood in 1976.

Fr. John earned a B.S., *Summa cum Laude* in Mathematics at Allentown College of St. Francis de Sales (now DeSales University). He also earned an M.A. in theology and philosophy from The Catholic University of America. After ordination, Fr. John taught religion at Salesianum School in Wilmington. In 1982, he received his Ph.D. in moral theology from The Catholic University of America.

During the 1980s, Fr. John served on the faculty and formation team at the Oblate Seminary in Washington, D.C. Later he served as religious superior and, in 1987, became president of the DeSales School of Theology. Fr. John also served as Executive Director of the Washington Theological Consortium.

From 2012 to 2017, he served as Executive Director of the Secretariat of Ecumenical and Inter-religious Affairs of the United States Conference of Catholic Bishops. During this time, Fr. Crossin was also a visiting fellow at the Woodstock Theological Center at Georgetown University, President of the North American Academy of Ecumenists, and a Consulter to the Pontifical Council for Promoting Christian Unity at the Vatican. He was a member of the

Pontifical Council's Team for the Joint Working Group with the World Council of Churches.

Fr. John then became Director of Spiritual Formation at the St. Luke Institute in Silver Spring, Maryland. Following this position, Fr. John had a research sabbatical during which he wrote his latest book, *Moving into the Ecumenical Future: Foundations of a Paradigm for Christian Ethics,* published in 2022.

Fr. John was a prolific and excellent writer. Many of the titles of his articles and books pertinent to the topics in his book are listed at the end of this guide.

Fr. John was recognized as a national leader in ecumenism. He received the Interfaith Bridge Builders Award of the Interfaith Conference of Metropolitan Washington, the Pillar of Faith Award of the Howard University School of Divinity United Church of Christ, and the Washington Theological Consortium Ecumenical Award. Fr. John was also a member of the Catholic Theological Society of America, The Society of Christian Ethics, and the Thomas Moore Society of Washington.

While in the Washington/Northern Virginia area, Fr. Crossin ministered at Annunciation Parish in the Archdiocese of Washington, Our Lady of Good Counsel Parish in Vienna, Virginia, and St. John Neumann Parish in Reston, Virginia.

Fr. John retired in Reston 2022 to focus on his writing and assist in the parish. He brought Salesian Spirituality into all his academic and pastoral work. He was passionate in exploring Christian faith and finding common ground with all faiths.

Fr. John, after a short illness, was reborn into eternal life on May 12, 2023. His Mass of Christian Burial was celebrated at St. John Neumann Catholic Church. The next day he was laid to rest in the Oblate Cemetery in Childs, Maryland.

Sources

- Oblate of St. Francis de Sales website: www.oblates.org
- The Catholic University of America Alumni Magazine, *Alumni Corner: In Memoriam*, Fall 2023, p. 32.

FR. CROSSIN'S PUBLICATIONS

- *Moving into the Ecumenical Future*
- *Walking in Virtue*
- *Everyday Virtues*
- *What Are They Saying About Virtue?*
- *Friendship: The Key to Spiritual Growth*

A Note from Loyes Spayd

MY STORY WITH FR. JOHN CROSSIN

I met Fr. John Crossin, OSFS, on a Cursillo weekend in December of 1984. He was the spiritual director on the retreat and I was going through a very difficult time in my life and was very much in need of spiritual help. He was extremely helpful, compassionate, and gentle! At that time, he offered to be my spiritual director. He directed me for a little more than a year then he had to move on to his position at the DeSales School of Theology. During this time with Fr. John, I learned about St. Francis de Sales and Salesian Spirituality. I did not realize during this time how much of an impact Salesian Spirituality would have on my life!

We saw each other at occasional events and shared our stories about books we were writing. I then took a position as Director of Religious Education at an Oblate parish, Our Lady of Good Counsel in Vienna, VA. and saw Fr. John more frequently at the parish and other Oblate events. I retired in 2010 and became a parishioner at another Oblate parish, St John Neumann in Reston, VA. I continued to see Fr. John on occasion. At St. John Neumann parish I continued to learn more about Salesian Spirituality and decided to become a Daughter of St. Francis de Sales and was consecrated on August 15, 2015. My formation and experience with the Daughters has been joyful and transformative. I realized then that God had been leading me to that point in my spiritual journey.

A few years later, guess who arrives at this parish? My dear friend, Fr. John, who, now retired, came to be in residence and finish his book, Moving into the Ecumenical Future: Foundations of a Paradigm for Christian Ethics. Before he had unpacked his bags, I asked him to once again be my spiritual director. Of course, being the generous priest he was, he said yes. In addition to being my director, we had many wonderful visits, lunches, dinners together and had many conversations about his book and his plans for the future of ecumenism described in his book.

For a short time before he became ill, Fr. John was the spiritual director of our local Daughters' group. In my last session with Fr. John, I made the comment that his future was going to be focused on making the "Future of ecumenism described in his book a reality." He grinned and said absolutely! I offered to write a review of his book on Amazon and to help in any way I could. Two weeks later Fr. John had passed on to eternal life.

As I mourned (and still do) the loss of Fr. John, I felt this need to help establish his vision but I had no idea how to start. I started making some contacts online, and met with Fr. Don Heet who had been a good friend of Fr. John and who has a lot of experience. Fr. Don, as I knew he would be, was extremely helpful and both of us started doing some research. In my online travels, Fr. John's brother, Bob, found me and asked me if I would like to join the Partnership Team whose membership included John's siblings, some Oblate priests, and some close friends and colleagues.

I was thrilled and, of course, said yes. I didn't have to do this all by myself, there was a community. That fact shouldn't have surprised me!!

I have now been on the team for several months and it is a wonderful experience. What a gifted and faith filled group! My latest contribution has been to write a Reading Guide to Fr. John's book, a tool I hope will be helpful to parishioners, book clubs, high schools, colleges, and seminaries and any interested Christians. The purpose of the Guide is not just to highlight and clarify important issues, but also, in a prayerful context, to reflect on the content: how does ecumenism affect my spiritual life and that of my faith community? What can I do to build the future envisioned in this book? You do not have to be a moral theologian or a scholar

A Note from Loyes Spayd

but as Christian sharing a desire for Christian Unity what can I do where I am. And, as I discovered again, you do not do this alone. There are faith communities out there who want the same thing. Connect with them!

When I started this project, I felt very overwhelmed and not sure I could do justice to Fr. John's book but I have not been alone. The Team, Fr. John's family, my faith community and my friends have supported and guided me. Most importantly, I have experienced the guidance of the Holy Spirit (and probably Fr. John's) in this work.

Fr. John was optimistic and hopeful! So am I and so will you be!

www.ingramcontent.com/pod-product-compliance
Lightning Source LLC
Chambersburg PA
CBHW072014060426
42446CB00043B/2540